Spanking Goals
& Toe Pokes
Football Sayings Explained

Tommy Martin

Proverse Hong Kong

Spanking Goals and Toe Pokes: Football Sayings Explained gathers together 800 or so expressions which have been used in English-language football commentaries over the past forty years or more.

Football commentary is a specialized art and football commentators need a gift of expression to complement their love and knowledge of football itself. They use a rich language, colloquial and metaphorical. Listeners need to learn to understand this quickly if they wish to follow football closely.

Football is now not only a world sport but the most popular sport in the world. One series of advertisements has claimed that it is a world language; a means of making friends without words. But football commentators do use words. And even non-native speakers of English enjoy or perhaps even prefer watching games when the commentary is given in English by knowledgable native speakers.

To make it possible for football fans to enjoy the game and English language commentaries to the full, Tommy Martin's *Spanking Goals and Toe Pokes: Football Sayings Explained* lists over 800 expressions which he has heard commentators use – all of them are idiomatic, colloquial, and/or metaphorical – and explains them in language that is more straightforward. Also included are some sayings used by footballers themselves.

An **index of key words** makes it easy for fans to find the sayings in the book which they have heard and want to understand. A **basic football vocabulary** is also included and this will be found very useful, particularly for new admirers of the game. A **note and diagram on the various positions** where players play is also provided for additional reference.

A series of **illustrations** shows what each of a number of these metaphorical sayings seems to say, if we interpret them literally. Amusing and witty in themselves, these illustrations prove the need for the explanations that this book gives.

Readers are welcome to submit more sayings to the publisher, Proverse Hong Kong. We may add your contribution to a new edition of this book.

Spanking Goals
&
Toe Pokes
Football Sayings Explained

by Tommy Martin

edited by Gillian Bickley
indexed by Verner Bickley
illustrations by Jacinta Read

Proverse Hong Kong

Spanking Goals and Toe Pokes: Football Sayings Explained
by Tommy Martin, 2008.
New edition published in paperback in Hong Kong by Proverse Hong Kong,
June 2017.
ISBN: 978-988-8228-27-0.
Availability includes from https://www.createspace.com/7246515
Original text, "Football Sayings and Meanings" & "Basic Football Vocabulary"
© T. J. Martin, June 2008.
This edition © Proverse Hong Kong June 2017.
First published in paperback in Hong Kong by Proverse Hong Kong, June 2008.
ISBN 978-988-99668-2-9
Edited by Gillian Bickley.
Illustrated by Jacinta Read.
Index by Verner Bickley.

Enquiries to:
Proverse Hong Kong, P.O. Box 259, Tung Chung Post Office, Tung Chung, NT,
Hong Kong SAR.
E-mail: proverse@netvigator.com Web site: www.proversepublishing.com

Moral Rights:
The right of Tommy J. Martin to be identified as the author of this book has been
asserted by him in accordance with the Copyright, Designs and Patents Act 1988.
The right of Verner Bickley to be identified as the author of "Index" has been
asserted by him in accordance with the Copyright, Designs and Patents Act 1988.
The right of Gillian Bickley to be identified as the editor of this book and author
of "Editor's note" has been asserted by her in accordance with the Copyright,
Designs and Patents Act 1988.
The right of Jacinta Read to be identified as the illustrator of this book has been
asserted by her in accordance with the Copyright, Designs and Patents Act 1988.
The right of John Dykes to be identified as the writer of the PRreface has been
asserted by him in accordance with the Copyright, Designs and Patents Act 1988.

Cover design by Proverse Hong Kong and Alan Chow
Cover illustrations by Jacinta Read.

Preface

Some years ago, I was fortunate enough to work as the host of ESPN STAR Sport's Asia-wide coverage of international cricket. In doing so I worked side-by-side with former England legend Geoffrey Boycott who was without rival when it came to delivering a string of pithy Yorkshire-accented observations in his role as expert summariser.

Visiting India one year on a fact-finding trip, I worked with a focus group of teenage boys in Delhi. I was startled to hear each of them slip into Boycott-speak whenever they had to offer a strong opinion. "That batsman's roo-beesh!" scoffed one. "Call that bowling?" said another, "my mother could have hit eet with a stick of rhubarb!"

The power of television, indeed. Whenever one of the Football Focus pundits offers a choice dose of "footyspeak" these days, I mentally roam Asia, picturing Thai youngsters yelling "man on!" during a kickabout, Malaysian kampong kids talking about "keeping it tight early doors" and a Hong Kong coach admitting that he's as "sick as a parrot".

Tommy Martin must have taken a similar mental flight of fancy while watching our exhaustive football coverage on his television. He is to be saluted for actually listening to our pundits long enough to take note of their favourite phrases. He is also to be saluted for his brave efforts to make linguistic sense of some of these *bons mots*, which have in some cases taken on a life all of their own.

Mind you, perhaps it all came easily to Tommy. After all, anyone who can make out what they're talking about up there on Tyneside should find translating "footyspeak" to be an absolute "walk in the park". Whatever that means. Enjoy the book!

John Dykes
Presenter, ESPN Star Sports' football coverage

Publishers' Acknowledgements

The Publishers gratefully acknowledge support from Dr Hari N. Harilela, GBS, OBE, JP.

We gratefully acknowledge help and/or sponsorship given by the individuals and organizations listed below:

China System Co. Ltd., Hong Kong. Hong Kong Baptist University: Professor Terry Yip (Department of English Language and Literature); Mr Danny Chow (Printing Section); Mr Henry So, Mr S. H. Tong (ITSC). P-Solution (HK) Ltd.

Author's Acknowledgements

Many friends and colleagues have encouraged and helped me with the sayings in this book, in particular my good friend Peter Quigley, Paul Truman my football colleague and good mate, and computer whiz Tony Dancaster.

I especially would like to thank Gillian and Verner Bickley for all their hard work and unremitting patience in putting this book together.

I warmly acknowledge the directors of Assumption College, Samut Prakarn, Thailand; Brother Sakda, Brother Vinai, and headmaster Master Thongban, for the strong support they give to football coaches and students at this excellent school.

Author's Dedication

This book is for "Crocket"
and all Geordie ex-pats all over the world.

Author's Introduction

I have heard people say the words and expressions in this book during the many, many years that I have loved football and been a part of the world of football. Having been a player in several countries and now a coach, I have taken them for granted and, as far as I remember, have never had any difficulty understanding what they mean.

But, since moving to live in out of Britain, I have discovered how difficult some football-lovers in other countries find it to understand what TV and radio commentators mean, when giving their commentaries on a game.

This book is my way of helping my friends and all those in Asia who love football, to understand football commentaries better and so enjoy them more.

All the words, phrases and expressions in this book, I have heard used, in one context or another.

In this book, I sometimes give a very specific explanation of what a word, phrase or expression meant in the context in which it was said when I made a note of it. The next time I hear the same words, or when you yourself hear them, the specific application of the basic meaning will very likely be different. But the underlying meaning will be similar. – Any use of language takes on its meaning from the context in which it is used, football commentaries included. – From reading through this book, you will get a good idea of the type of language used in football commentaries. You will see the underlying meaning of the words and expressions and you will see specific applications of the phraseology. You will see how to apply your knowledge of the examples in the book to the commentaries that you hear in the future. I suggest you keep this book by you as a reference, for whenever you hear a fresh word, phrase or expression that you find puzzling.

By the way, quite a few of the phrases are used in

familiar, colloquial British conversation, quite unrelated to football as well!

All of these sayings have been used at some time or other by the television commentators and other football experts. Some of the phrases in this book go back to the 70s and 80s and many of them are still used today. Most British people will have no problem understanding them. Many of the words and phrases come from many different British dialects and regions, and some are in what we can call jargon or slang. book will try to explain as many as them as we can in a humorous way.

This book is for people who love watching football on television and / or listening to radio commentaries, and who would like some explanation of the meaning of some of the words and phrases which they hear, and which they certainly did not learn in school.

I hope you have fun reading and remembering them.

T. J. Martin
2008.

It takes two to tango.

Editor's note

Readers will find the vividness of the language used in Tommy Martin's *Spanking Goals and Toe Pokes: Football Sayings Explained* very striking. Also striking is the extent to which the language borrows images from other modern sports – sports such as archery, boxing, cycling, fencing, game-shooting, horse-racing, horse-riding, marksmanship, sailing and swimming – as well as from medieval sports such as jousting. The sayings also use language from many other types of civilian human activity: – accounting, acrobatics, agriculture, ballroom-dancing, body-building, bull-fighting, card-playing, carpentry, cooking, diamond-cutting, dog-fighting, capital punishment, fish-mongering, foot-soldiering, gambling, gardening, gold-mining, milling, mining, motoring, sewing, steam-railway transport, theatricals (including show-boat theatricals) and walking. There is also language from warfare ancient and modern, both old world and new world style (taking scalps), as well as the language of territorial conquest (barbarian invasions). Vocabulary is borrowed from animal behaviour ("mauling", and "tooth and nail" fighting (bears, lions, etc.), "barking up a tree" (dogs) and "ruling the roost" (cockerels)).

We can also find among these sayings quotations from the Bible ("He threaded that ball through the eye of a needle") and from well-known literature, such as R. L. Stevenson's famous and often-quoted story, *Dr Jekyll and Mr. Hyde*.

In other words, the sayings used by football commentators and others interested in football reflect the reading and interests of the speakers. It is not surprising if those who do not share the same interests, as well as those who have not done the same reading, may take a little time to warm up to the language used by any particular speaker, just as it takes a crossword-puzzle enthusiast time to get used to the style of a particular puzzle-compiler.

Apart from these features, the language used both in the sayings and by Tommy Martin in his explanations and commentary, is often highly colloquial. Although grammatical, it most likely goes far beyond the types of expression taught in a normal class-room. Certainly, most native-speakers of English will understand what is meant (although we remember that not all those who met Eliza Dolittle in G. B. Shaw's play *Pygmalion* and its film adaptation, *My Fair Lady*, when she first entered "polite" society, understood her when she spoke colloquially). And those that do understand this colloquial language may never use it themselves.

Again referring to the example given by Eliza Dolittle, we remember the scene where she urges on a horse which is carrying her bet, in language which one lady certainly understands, because she faints with horror when she hears it. Certainly, this lady will never use it herself. Others – less easily upset – may use the language, but in highly specific and well-understood contexts, when speaking to or among particular groups of people.

Spanking Goals and Toe Pokes: Football Sayings Explained provides useful and necessary information to football enthusiasts world-wide in an interesting and succinct way. The general reader, also, interested in extending his or her knowledge of colloquial English, will find it valuable. For everyone, it provides a most useful object lesson in the mental gymnastics that language requires of us all.

Gillian Bickley
2008

Table of contents

He bagged a brace.

He can turn on a sixpence.

Table of illustrations and diagrams

He carved out a good chance.

He has to bite the bullet on this one.

Football sayings and meanings

Expressions.	Meanings in the original contexts.
a derby game	A match between two teams who are arch rivals or are from the same city. For example: Liverpool versus (vs) Everton, Newcastle vs Sunderland, Manchester United vs Manchester City.
A penalty shoot-out looks on the cards.	If a match is still level after extra time, the teams will have to take penalty kicks to decide the match.
a prolific goal-scorer	a striker who normally scores many goals each season
a toss up; a flip of the coin	The captains of the two teams throw / toss / flip a coin to decide who gets what side of the field or who gets the kick-off.
against all the odds	unexpectedly (adv.); unexpected (adj.)
against the run of play	A team which has been defending most of the game has broken away and scored a goal.
As long as they keep their heads they might win this.	If team members do not lose their tempers and do not get any of their players sent off, the team could win the match.
At the end of the day, they just weren't good enough.	A team has been beaten because the other team was stronger and better.
attacking the ball from the corner kick	moving fast and hard towards the ball to try to score, after a kick from a corner of the field has been made
Both teams are up	Both teams are confident of winning

15

for it.	and are ready to try their best to win.
box, the six-yard box	the area in front of the goal where the goal kicks are taken from
Chelsea looms.	A team must play a leader in the league or another very good team very soon.
danger area	goal-keeper's box, penalty area
from the grass roots	from a lowly position
hard going	difficult
He always gets the job done.	A player always plays well in the position to which he has been assigned.
He bagged a brace.*	A player has just scored two goals.
He ballooned that one over the bar.	A player kicked the ball at the goal but it went high over the top of the crossbar.
He bent the ball into the top corner.	The player made the ball swerve round the defensive wall of players and into the top corner of the goal.
He blew that one.	A player might have missed an easy chance or a penalty kick or the goal-keeper might have let in a goal.
He blocked it very well.	A player got in front of a shot and stopped it with his foot or body.
He brought it down very well.	A player controlled the ball very well as it was in the air.
He burst the net with that one.	A player has just scored a very good goal with a very powerful shot.
He can take a bow for that one.*	A player has just scored a very good goal and is applauded by the crowd.
He can turn on a sixpence.*	A player is able to turn his body rapidly and skilfully.
He can win the game for them if	A player is very skilfull and if he starts to play well his team could win the

16

he turns it on.	game.
He carved out a good chance.*	A player has created a good chance for himself to score a goal.
He caught him on the shin.	The defender kicked him in the shin (leg).
He caught him with his elbow.	A player, when challenged for the ball, was hit in the face or head by the other player's elbow.
He caught that one right on the button.	A player got hit in the face (on his nose button, i.e. his nose) with the ball.
He clattered him.	A player tackled someone very hard and perhaps fouled him and knocked him over.
He climbed all over him.	1) The player jumped on the back of an opponent trying to head the ball. OR 2) He defeated the opposing player very easily.
He climbed high for that ball.	The player jumped very high to head the ball.
He clipped the back of his heels.	A player kicked an opponent on the heels from behind.
He completely miss-hit that one	A player tried to hit a ball and missed it completely.
He could be gone for that tackle.	A player tackled very badly and could be sent off for having committed a foul.
He couldn't give a monkey's.	A coach, manager or player does not care what happens.
He couldn't hit a barn door.	A player seems incapable of scoring a goal (because he has missed the goal many times during the game).
He couldn't score if his life depended on it.	A player is not very good at scoring goals.

He couldn't tie his boot laces.	A player will never be as good as the other one he is playing against.
He couldn't trap a bag of cement.	A player is very unskilled and cannot get the ball under control.
He curved that round the wall.	A player took a shot at the goal from a free kick and bent the ball (swerved it) round all the players who were defending.
He cut his way through the defense.	A player dribbled through the defense very well.
He dealt with that very well.	A player coped (did) very well, e.g. with a very difficult pass. / OR The keeper responded very well to a high cross.
He doesn't know what day it is.	A player who has been hurt or knocked out doesn't know what's happening.
He doesn't seem to have any pre-match nerves.	The player looks and is calm and collected before a game.
He doesn't want to get in a foot race with him.	A player should not try to out-run a certain player as the other player is very fast.
He doesn't want to know.	A player is just not trying. He's having a bad game and looks as if he doesn't wish to continue to play.
He drilled it into the bottom corner. / He smashed it into the bottom corner.	A player shot the ball past the goal-keeper into the bottom corner of the net very hard and fast.
He drills through the ball very well.	A player can kick the ball very hard with very good technique, making the ball go very fast.
He dropped a right	A player / the goal-keeper has made a

clanger.	very bad mistake.
He dropped his shoulder and waltzed past him.	A player just ran or dribbled past an opponent and made it look very easy.
He fancies his chances now.	A player who is playing well thinks he can score / is very confident.
He fell over his own feet.	A player who has the ball at his feet fell over when no-one was near him.
He floated the ball into the danger area.	He kicked the ball high into the goal-keeper's box.
He fluffed it.	A player made a mess of something. E.g. he was given a good pass in front of the goal but missed the goal.
He fought tooth and nail for that ball.	A player was very determined to win the ball from the other player.
He gets them psyched up / all fired up for it [the game].	A coach who can excite his players and get them motivated.
He goes to ground too easily.	He's a player who falls over whenever he is tackled.
He got a whack in the face.	A player got hit in the face (e.g. by a boot or an arm).
He got on the end of that one.	A player headed the ball from a cross (a ball kicked cross-ways across the pitch).
He got stuck into it.	The player tackled very hard and worked very hard in the match.
He got the rub of the green.	A player might have got a bit lucky with a pass or bounce.
He had a bit of a stab at that one.	A player made a cursory attempt to shoot the ball.

He had a rush of blood.	He did something stupid and made a mistake.
He had a touch of the collywobbles.	A player has made a very basic mistake, which is unusual for him.
He had an absolute blinder.	A player had a brilliant match.
He had the guts to have a go at it.	A player has just tried to score from a difficult position.
He has a good first touch.	A player has excellent control of the ball when it comes to him.
He has a lot of pace.	A player can run very quickly.
He has a new lease of life now.	A player who previously looked as though he was tired has started to play very well.
He has a niggling injury.	A player has an injury which keeps coming back.
He has a quick change of pace / burst of speed.	That player is very good at quick acceleration.
He has a touch of the jitters.	The player is a bit nervous.
He has an old head on young shoulders.	He is a very good and composed young player, who's playing as if he's much more experienced than he is.
He has bags and bags of ability.	A player has lots of skill and is a great player.
He has claimed the goal. The ball took a deflection.	The player shot the ball at the goal. It hit one of the opposing players but still went in the net. The player is claiming it for himself.
He has good presence of mind.	He's a very good player, who has the ability to make good decisions during a game.

He has great technique.	A player is very skilfull and technically gifted.
He has moulded his team around him.	A coach or manager has built his team around a particular very good player.
He has oceans of space.	A player is in a very good position on the field with lots of room.
He has that never-say-die attitude.	He's a player who never gives up even when there may not be much chance of winning the game.
He has the big guns on now.	A coach or manager has put his best players on the field to try to win the game.
He has to bite the bullet on this one.	A player must accept the decision, get on with the game and keep his opinion to himself.
He has to hit the back of the net	A player has a good chance to score.
He has to take it on the chin.	A player, who has been criticized, has to accept it and get on with the game.
He has tremendous presence.	He's a great player whom every-one admires. / He is a great leader.
He has very quick feet.	A player is very good at dribbling.
He hasn't a clue what he's doing.	A player is not very good, or is having a very bad game.
He hasn't given him a sniff all day.	A defender, who is marking an opponent, is not letting the player have much of the ball.
He held his ground.	A player did not move when challenged for the ball.
He hooked the ball over the bar.	The player has just missed the goal from a very close position and kicked it over the cross bar.

He is the backbone of the team.	A player is a good, solid, dependable player and holds the team together.
He just doesn't cut the mustard for me.	In my view, a certain player isn't very good and shouldn't be in a particular team.
He just ghosts in at the back post.	A player gets in a good position to score at the back post without being seen by the defenders.
He just nicked it.	A player stole the ball from an opponent just as he was going to pass or shoot.
He just takes it in his stride.	The player doesn't panic and makes everything look very easy.
He keeps backing in to him.	A player keeps pushing backwards on to an opposing player, who is marking him.
He keeps banging them in, week in and week out.	A player keeps scoring goals each time he plays.
He keeps chopping and changing the defense.	The coach or manager keeps changing his defensive line-up each week.
He keeps committing himself.	A defender commits himself to a plan of action with the result that an opposing player might be able to run past him.
He keeps getting on the blind side of him.	A player keeps getting the better of a defender by coming in behind him, so he cannot see him or the ball.
He keeps getting on the end of the crosses.	A player is very good at jumping up to head the ball, when it is being kicked cross-ways across the pitch.
He keeps giving it away.	A player keeps making bad passes and the ball keeps going to the opponents.
He keeps giving	A player keeps losing the ball too

the ball away too cheaply.	easily.
He keeps giving the Ref. verbal.	A player keeps arguing with the referee.
He keeps going down the flanks.	A player keeps running down the wings (the sides of the field of play).
He keeps leading with the elbow.	A player keeps jumping for the ball, putting his elbow out first and perhaps hitting an opponent with it.
He keeps leaving his foot in.	When a player challenges for the ball he tries to injure the other player.
He keeps playing the ball into no-man's land.	A player keeps passing long balls where none of his team-mates are and so they cannot reach them.
He keeps playing the ball square.	The player passes the ball sideways and not forward.
He keeps pushing his luck with the referee.	A player keeps arguing with the referee and he might get a yellow or red card for doing so.
He keeps squandering chances.	A player keeps missing easy chances.
He keeps steaming in and missing the challenge.	A player keeps running in too fast after the ball or another player.
He kept a clean sheet.	The goal-keeper did not concede any goals.
He leads by example.	He's a very good player – probably the captain – and he always plays fair and is a good example for young players to follow.
He let fly with that one.	A player hit a very hard shot at the goal.
He lobbed it over	A player has scored a goal by kicking

the keeper's head.	it high over the goal-keeper's head.
He looks absolutely shattered.	A player, who has played very hard, run all over the field and given his all, is exhausted.
He looks like he has two left feet.*	A player is not having a good game and he keeps falling over.
He looks lost in midfield.	A player is not playing very well in the centre of the field.
He looks lost in that position.	A player is not playing well in a certain position and is having a bad game.
He made a complete hash of that.	A player made a very bad mistake. E.g. he missed the goal or made a very bad tackle.
He made a jinking run.	A player dribbled past an opponent very fast and skilfully.
He made a nuisance of himself.	A player – normally a striker – fought very hard and used his physical presence to put the defenders under pressure and forced them to make mistakes.
He made no contact with him.	It looked like a foul but really the player did not connect with or foul his opponent.
He makes them tick.	He makes the team as a whole play very well. He is their best player.
He marked him out of the game.	A defender had a great game by not letting the forward, whom he is playing against, get the better of him.
He missed a right sitter.	The player missed a great opportunity in front of the goal.
He must act before the transfer window closes.	A coach wishing to lose or obtain a player must do it quickly before the transfer deadline expires.

He must bury that one.	The player has an easy chance to score and should hit the net.
He must hit the target more often.	A player who keeps shooting and missing must shoot more successfully.
He needs time to settle in this team.	A player, who has just joined the team, needs some time to get used to playing with his new team-mates and their system.
He needs to cover ground more quickly.	A player looks very slow.
He needs to prove his worth.	A new player, whom a team might just have bought, has to start playing well, so as to justify his move to the new club.
He needs to pull his finger out.	A player, who is not playing very well, must start playing better.
He needs to pull the trigger early.	A player waits too long to shoot in front of the goal. He should do it earlier.
He needs to put his cards on the table.	A coach (or manager) should let people know what he is going to do / what his intentions are.
He needs to recharge his batteries.	A player looks very tired and needs to rest.
He needs to stay on his feet.	A player keeps falling down or slipping.
He needs to step up to the plate.	A player needs to take responsibility for the task; for example, to take a penalty kick.
He needs to stop pussy-footing around.	A player needs to start playing better. E.g. perhaps he should pass the ball better.
He needs to take	A player is only looking straight ahead

the blinkers off.	and is not looking around him for better opportunities to pass to someone who might be in a better position to score than he is.
He needs to take the bull by the horns.	A player needs to assert himself in the game.
He needs to wake up and smell the roses.*	A player thinks things are going well for him, but really they are not going well and he's fooling (deceiving) himself.
He never gets flustered.	The player is very steady and composed under pressure.
He never gets the better of him!	A player keeps trying to get past an opponent but cannot do it.
He never got a sniff of [or "a sniff at"] that one.	The keeper got beaten by a very fast shot. / A goal-keeper has just let in a really fast hard shot and didn't get close to stopping it.
He never moans but just gets on with it.	A player never complains when fouled.
He never put a foot wrong in the game.	A player was outstanding and played very well indeed.
He never really had his heart in the game.	A player never looked as though he was trying very hard throughout the game.
He never stops whinging.	A player is always complaining or moaning.
He over-hit that.	A player passed a ball too hard for his team-mate to catch.
He peeled off him.	A player turned and moved away from his marker very quickly.
He picked up a little knock.	A player has been tackled or hit and has a slight injury.

He pinged that one in.	A player has made a very good, fast, strong and accurate straight pass to one of his team-mates or at the goal.
He played for the penalty. He dived in the box.	The player deliberately fell over in the penalty box looking for a penalty.
He played the man not the ball. A Foul.	The defender tackled the opponent and did not go for the ball.
He plays in the heart of the defense.	A player plays in the middle of the defence.
He provides the ammunition for the strikers.	A player supplies the passes for the forwards so that they can score.
He pulled off a great save.	The goal-keeper stopped a strong shot at the goal.
He put it on a plate for him.	A player made a good pass to his team-mate right in front of the goal.
He put that away.	He scored a goal.
He ran himself into the ground.	The player never stopped running for the whole game and was exhausted at the end.
He reads the game very well.	A player is very good and knows most of the strategy and techniques used in the game.
He really puts himself about.	A player is a very good tackler, very strong, and covers a lot of ground.
He really thumped that one.	A player kicked the ball very hard and with great strength.
He seems to have his head in the clouds.*	A player is not concentrating on his game, and is not playing well.
He sent the ball	The player kicked the ball hard and

into the stands.	high into the stadium.
He shadowed him everywhere he went on the park.	A player – i.e. a defender – marked a certain player and followed him wherever he went on the pitch.
He shanked that one.	A player kicked the ball but he mis-timed it and it did not go where he intended it to go.
He should	It is his duty to . . .. OR It is inevitable that he will . . ..
He should hang up his boots.	A player should retire from the game. He's too old to play.
He should never say "never".	A player should keep on trying.
He skied it.	A player(, who was in front of the goal,) kicked the ball high (over the bar).
He slotted it home.	A player scored a very good goal, beating the goal-keeper.
He snatched at it.	A player, who should have taken more time to shoot, panicked and missed the shot.
He sold the defender a right dummy.	The forward pretended to control the ball but let it go past him, fooling the defender.
He split the defense with that one.	A player made a very good pass through the defense to his team-mate.
He spooned that one over the bar.	A player kicked the ball over the bar from very close range.
He stuck to him like glue all game.	A defender marked a player throughout the game, never letting him get very far away from him.
He swivelled his hips, and left the	A player made a very good move and got past a particular defender.

defender standing.

He takes him on all the time.	A player keeps dribbling and tries to get past the defender.
He takes no prisoners, that one.	A player is a very hard tackler and never afraid.
He thinks he rules the roost.	A player thinks he is the best of all the players on the field.
He thinks he's hard done by.	This may be said, for example, when a player who has been fouled feels disgruntled because the referee didn't give him a free kick.
He thinks the other coach has stabbed him in the back.	He thinks that another coach has been saying things about him that were very damaging (e.g. made him lose his job).
He thinks two or three passes ahead of them.	A player is very intelligent and reads the game much better that the other players.
He thought all his birthdays had come at once.	A player was given a great chance to score when he did not expect to do so.
He thought he had all the time in the world.	A player was too slow. (E.g. he thought no-one was marking him; he was tackled and the ball was taken from him.)
He threaded that ball through the eye of a needle.	A player made a very good pass between two defenders.
He timed his run to perfection.	A player made a very good run towards the opposing goal.
He took his eye off the ball.	A player took his eyes off the ball just for a second and missed a chance. (E.g. when trying to score, and so missed the goal.)
He took the pace / the sting out of it	A player got the ball to stop /got the ball under control, as it was coming

[i.e. the ball].	towards him at a very fast pace / speed.
He tried his heart out.	The player never stopped trying to win the game.
He turned the defender inside out.	A player (e.g. the right-winger) made the defender look really poor by dribbling very fast and making him lose balance. E.g. "Manchester United winger Ronaldo turned Bolton full-back Campo inside out."
He unleashed one there.	A player has just hit a very hard shot at the goal.
He upended him there.	A player has just tackled an opponent and the opponent has been thrown up in the air.
He wants too many touches on the ball	A player keeps losing the ball, as he keeps the ball too long and gets it taken from him.
He was (OR "was caught") in two minds [with that one].	A player (who had a chance to score or pass) didn't make his mind up quickly enough [as to how to play the ball].
He was a mile off-side.	A player was well off-side.
He was ball watching.	A player wasn't concentrating on watching his opponent, but watching the ball instead, and this let his opponent get behind him and score.
He was bundled off the ball.	A player was pushed off the ball / was fouled and fell over.
He was caught flat-footed.	A defender was beaten, caught off-balance.
He was chopped from behind.	A player was tackled from behind and fouled.
He was completely bamboozled.	A player was completely fooled by an opponent.

He was in the right place at the right time.	A player scored a goal by being in a good position at the time a pass was made to him.
He was in two minds whether to come for that one.	A goal-keeper was very hesitant about coming out to catch the ball. He started to come out, but then changed his mind.
He was just a flash in the pan.	A player, who started out playing very well, soon showed that he is not that good after all.
He was sandwiched.	A player was fouled, by being squashed in the middle between two defenders.
He was wide open. / He had acres of room.	A player was in a good position to score but his team-mate did not pass to him.
He whipped in a great ball.	A player kicked the ball very hard, curling it into the box.
He whipped that one into the danger area.	He hit a very fast and hard ball into the goal-keeper's box.
He will be in hot water with the coach over that.	A player will be in trouble for doing something bad: e.g. getting sent off, giving away a penalty.
He will be kicking himself for that miss.	A player who has just missed a very easy chance will be very hard on himself / will criticize himself severely for missing the chance.
He will bide his time and get him back / get back at him.	A player who was fouled or kicked will wait for a chance to do the same to the player who did it.
He will feel that in the morning.	A player, who has been bruised or injured, will feel more pain the next day.

He will get found out in the end.	A player, who is playing in a certain position that doesn't suit him / OR, who is not very good, will eventually make a noticeable mistake.
He will get some right stick for that.	A player will be ridiculed for making a bad mistake or a bad tackle. / A coach will be ridiculed for saying or doing the wrong thing.
He will have a right go at them in the dressing room.	The coach or manager is very unhappy with his team's performance and will reprimand them at half time, or at the end of the game.
He will have his job cut out to keep him in check.	A player – probably a defender – will have a hard time marking an opposing player, since the opponent is a very good player.
He will never live that down.	A player who has made a very bad mistake will never forget it because others will keep on reminding him about it.
He will take the spot kick.	A player will come and take a penalty kick.
He will terrorize the defense.	A player who is a very good forward will run at the defenders and dribble and cause many problems for them.
He wishes he could turn back the clock.	A player is getting too old and knows he will never be as good as he used to be, when he was young.
He won't make any friends by saying that.	A coach, manager or player has made unacceptable comments about a team, or a player, or club.
He won't make many friends by doing that.	A player might be doing something very bad and will be thought of very badly.
He won't play	He wants to take the lead / to be

second fiddle to any one / him.	thought better than everyone else / than a particular person.
He won't sleep tonight after that.	A player has done something he regrets: e.g. he might have missed a very easy chance to score. As a result he will continually think about what happened and this may stop him from sleeping when he goes to bed.
He would march into hell for this team.	This player never stops trying and will always give of his best.
He's a bit of a flapper.	A player is a worrier and panics (e.g. when he has the ball).
He's a bit too clever for his own good.	A player was trying some difficult or different skills or techniques, but they did not work out (i.e. they were not successful).
He's a box-to-box player.	A player is very fit and will run the whole field to score a goal and then run back to help defend.
He's a busy little player.	A player is very active in the game; always moving and running.
He's a dead-ball specialist.	A player is very good at taking free kicks, penalties and corners.
He's a flare player.	A player is very exciting and skilfull.
He's a good finisher.	The player is very good at scoring goals.
He's a hit-and-miss player.	A player is not very consistent.
He's a key player in their team.	A player is one of their best players.
He's a liability to the team.	A player is not very good and could make his team lose the game.
He's a little rusty.	A player, who is not playing to his

	normal standard, might have just come back to join the team, e.g. after an injury.
He's a nippy little player.	A slightly-built player is very skilfull and fast.
He's a no nonsense type of player.	A player is a very hard, strong-minded player and just gets on with the game.
He's a notch above every one else.	A player is much better than all the other players on the pitch.
He's a quality player.	He's a very good player; one of the best.
He's a real bread-and-butter player.	A player is not the most skilfull or exciting player but he plays a useful steady game and is a good team-member.
He's a right nutter that one.	A player has a bad temper / does stupid things on the pitch.
He's a right time-waster.	A player is trying to keep the ball away from the opponents at the end of the game, with only minutes to go (e.g. by keeping the ball near the corner flag).
He's a show-stopper.	A player is fantastic; a great player.
He's a thorn in his side, that one.	A certain player is marking another player and not letting him play his normal game.
He's a very greedy / selfish player.	He's a player who will not pass to his team-mates (who might be in a better position to score than him) / OR he dribbles too much.
He's a very level-headed player.	A player is very calm and intelligent.
He's a very mamby-pamby player.	A player is very soft; always falling down or getting hurt.

He's a wily old fox.*	A player is getting old but is still very good. He knows all the tricks and nothing gets past him.
He's absolutely gutted.	A player is dejected and depressed for a range of possible reasons; perhaps at the way he played, or because he missed a great chance to score, or because his team lost the match.
He's already got the monkey on his back to start with.	A coach or manager is already under a lot of pressure and does not need any more problems to worry about.
He's always the first on the team sheet.	This player is the one whom the manager thinks is his most influential or best player and he is always selected to play in the game.
He's an impact player.	He's a very important player in the team and can win the game for them if he plays well.
He's as daft as a brush.	A player is always joking OR is a very funny character.
He's as hard as nails.	The player is very strong and never afraid of anyone.
He's back in the fold again.	A player, who previously was dropped from the squad, is playing better and is now back in the team.
He's bang in form now.	A player played very well in all his recent games and is playing well in this one as well.
He's barking up the wrong tree with him.	A player is not taking the correct approach. For example, he is arguing either with a referee, who has a reputation as a strict disciplinarian, or he is arguing with a very hard player. He will come out the worse for it.
He's been misfiring	A player, who's normally very good at

35

lately.	shooting goals, keeps missing the target.
He's been thrown in (OR "thrown right in") at the deep end.	A player (e.g. a young player who hasn't played before) has been picked to play in a big match. / A young inexperienced player has been brought into the team – perhaps because one of the regular players has been injured – and he has to play in the missing player's position against a good team.
He's bottled it.	A player has backed out of a challenge [because he was afraid].
He's busting a gut to get to that ball.	A player is trying very hard to get to a pass from his team-mate.
He's chasing shadows all the game.	A player is not playing very well.
He's close to double figures this season.	A player has scored perhaps nine goals and is now trying to get to ten or more.
He's cock-a-hoop now.	A player who has just scored a goal is very happy and pleased with himself.
He's come back to haunt them.	A team has just sold a player to a certain team and he has just scored a goal against his former team.
He's done all the donkey-work.	A player has run and worked very hard for his team.
He's given his all.	A player has worked hard and tried his best in a match.
He's giving him a right roasting.	A player (a forward) keeps going past a defender for most of the game.
He's going to have a crack at it.	A player looks like he is lining himself up to try to score from a free kick with a hard shot.

He's going to have a go. / He's going to take it on.	A player is getting ready to shoot at the goal (i.e. from a free kick).
He's gone from hero to zero in ten minutes.	A player, who has just scored a goal, made a bad mistake soon after, and as a result, the opposition scored. People's feelings about him have thus changed very quickly, from high praise to strong disappointment.
He's gone right off the boil.	A good player is not playing up to his normal standard.
He's good at dealing with high balls.	A player is good at heading. / A goal-keeper is good at catching high balls into the box.
He's good at jockeying for the ball.	A defender holds his ground and does not commit himself.
He's good at the heart of the defense.	A player is good at playing in the middle of the defense.
He's got a flea in his ear.	A player or coach is complaining about something.
He's got a good pedigree.	A player or coach has been at many good clubs / is a very good professional.
He's got a lot of baggage.	A player's been involved in a whole lot of negotiations / complicated situations before joining a new team.
He's got a second bite at the cherry.	A player who has just missed a chance gets another opportunity to score.
He's got a sweet left foot.	A player is very skilfull at kicking the ball with his left foot.
He's got great technique.	A player is very good.
He's got his	A player has been sent off the pitch by

marching orders.	the referee.
He's got his shooting boots on now.	A player who might have been shooting poorly in the game has finally started to shoot better OR he has scored a goal.
He's got nerves of steel.	A player never panics under pressure and is very calm.
He's got nothing to show for that.	A player made a good run or pass but it didn't have any positive result.
He's got that in his locker.	A very good player can come up with something special when he needs too.
He's got the heart of a lion.	He's fearless and strong.
He's gutted.	A player is absolutely disappointed, with himself perhaps, or because his team has just lost a game.
He's having a lean spell.	A good player is not playing up to his normal standard.
He's having a right wobbler.	A player is getting very upset at someone.
He's having a stormer.	A player is playing brilliantly.
He's hit the nail on the head.	A manger or coach has said something about the game or about a player, which is absolutely correct.
He's in his comfort zone.	A player is well suited to his position and is comfortable there.
He's itching to get on the score sheet.	A player is trying very hard to score a goal for his team.
He's just scored a perfect hat trick.	A perfect hat trick is when a player scores three goals, one with the right foot, one with the left foot, and one with the head.
He's just switched	A player, who has been playing very

off now.*	well most of the game, is not playing very well now.
He's kept a clean sheet.	A goal-keeper has not conceded a goal in the match.
He's kicking the living daylights out of him.	A player is fouling an opposing player very badly, kicking him hard and repeatedly.
He's learning the tricks of the trade.	A young player is starting to play better by playing with more experienced players.
He's like a fish out of water in that position.	A player is having a bad game, playing in a position where he normally doesn't play.
He's limped off the park.	A player has been injured or hurt and has had to come off the field.
He's locking horns with him now.	A player is having a fight or argument with another player.
He's lost the plot now.	A player has lost control in some way. He may have lost his temper and hit an opponent and as a result got sent off; or he may have done something else very bad.
He's lurking with intent.	A player is hanging around (i.e. keeping close to) the goal, trying to find an opportunity to score.
He's made a right monkey out of him.	A player has played very well against an opponent and made him look very foolish.
He's marked him out of the game.	A defender has stopped an opponent from scoring or making (OR "creating") any chances by marking him very closely.
He's menacing in the air.	A player is very good at jumping for the ball and using his head.
He's mixing it up	A player is working very hard and

in the middle of the park.	creating very hard challenges to win the ball in midfield.
He's mopping up at the back.	A player – perhaps a sweeper – is picking up all the loose balls and having a good game.
He's nicked it off him.	A player has stolen the ball from another player.
He's not good enough to tie his boot laces.	One player is not nearly as good as another particular player. For example, a new player, who might just have joined a club, is not nearly as good as the player he replaced.
He's not much to write home about.	A player isn't very good-looking / is not much of a player.
He's not really been tested yet.	A goal-keeper has not yet had any shots taken at him, so we don't and can't yet know how good he is.
He's on fire today.*	A player is very fast and is playing very well.
He's one of the dark horses.	A player is not very well known but could very well become a good player and could surprise everyone one day.
He's only a one-footed player.	A certain player is only good with one foot (either the right or the left).
He's out cold.	A player has been knocked out. He's injured and unconscious.
He's over the hill. / He's past it.	A player is getting too old to play. He needs to retire.
He's picked up a knock.	A player has been injured.
He's put his head on the block now.	A coach or manager has made a comment or decision, which could make him lose his job if it does not work out.

He's ruined the party for them now.	A player has just scored a goal to make the score level, at a time when the other team thought they had won the match.
He's run himself right into trouble.	A player had the ball and – instead of passing or shooting – kept it and lost it.
He's run his socks off. He's run himself into the ground.	A player has run all over the pitch and never given up. He tried his best for the team.
He's running around like a headless chicken.	A player is playing very badly and is chasing the ball madly.
He's shot himself in the foot there.	A player made a very bad mistake.
He's show-boating now.	A player is doing tricks and showing off his skills to the supporters.
He's showing him too much of the ball.	The forward is letting the ball get too far in front of him, giving the defender the opportunity to take it from him.
He's sitting just in front of the back four.	A player is playing in a position immediately in front of the defense.
He's sneaked in at the back post.	A player has come in to score a goal at the far post behind the defenders.
He's so easy on the eye.	A player is very good to watch; a very good player.
He's spat out the dummy now.*	A player is getting upset and is acting like a little child throwing a tantrum.
He's spitting blood.	A player is very upset at something or someone.
He's still a bit rusty.	A player is out of practice and not playing very well.
He's stitched him	A player is marking another so closely

right up.	that he can't be effective.
He's taken a right knock there. He has got to shake it off / run it off.	A player has picked up an injury and must keep moving so it does not stiffen up.
He's taken over the reins.	A new coach or manager has come to the club and is now in charge.
He's taking the micky.	A player is doing tricks and taunting an opponent, trying to make fun of him.
He's the anchor-man of this team.	He's a very good player (e.g. the captain) who helps the team to play well.
He's the back-bone of this team.	A player is very strong and holds the team together; normally the centre half.
He's the midfield lynch-pin.	He's a very good midfield player who holds his team together.
He's the team's midfield dynamo.	The player is a great midfield player who never gives up.
He's too hot to handle.	A certain player is very good and will cause the defense many problems.
He's turned out to be a right lemon.*	A player whom a team bought has not played very well and was a bad buy. Not a good player.
He's unlocked the defense with that pass.	A player has made a very good pass through the defense to his team-mate, giving him a good opportunity to score.
He's very calm and collected.	A player is a very good steady player under pressure.
He's very cool under pressure.	He's a very composed player and never panics.
He's very good at nodding it down.	A player is very good at heading the ball down to his team-mates.
He's very good on	A tall player who looks unbalanced is

the deck for a big gangly lad.	really very skilfull.
He's very hard to knock off the ball.	He's a player who is very strong and not pushed off the ball easily.
He's very injury-prone.	The player is always getting injured.
He's very up and down.	He's an inconsistent player.
He's walking a tightrope out there.*	A player might be very close to getting a yellow or red card from the referee.
He's way out of order.	A player should not have done something (e.g. he should not have hit an opponent).
He's wrong-footed the goal-keeper.	A player has just taken a penalty kick. He sent the goal-keeper the wrong way and scored.
His arms are like windmills. They're all over the place.	A player is running or jumping for the ball, swinging his arms. (In consequence, he is very dangerous.)
His bark is worse than his bite.	What a certain coach says gives a worse impression of his temper than is really the case.
His celebrating is a bit over the top.	A player is celebrating having just scored a goal by doing something like a dance or jumping into the crowd. The speaker thinks this is exaggerated behaviour.
His feet looked rooted to the spot.	He didn't move quickly enough. E.g. The keeper was beaten easily.
His first touch let him down.	A player was unable to control the ball or pass with his first touch. As a result, he lost precious time or even possession.
His legs have gone.	He can't run any more. His legs have

	cramped up. He's too tired.
His reputation precedes him.	He's a great player whom everyone knows.
His reputation speaks for itself.	Every-one knows who he is. He's an outstanding player.
I bet he wishes the ground would open up and swallow him for that miss.	A player has just missed a very easy chance to score a goal and he must be devastated.
I don't think he will lose any sleep over it.	A player or coach won't worry very much about something.
I take my hat off to them.	A team has played a very good game.
I think he's seeing stars.	A player who has been hit on the head is dazed.
I think it's curtains for them now.	One team is being beaten and it looks as if they have no chance now to win.
I would have put money on him to put that away.	The speaker was certain a player would score, but he was wrong. The player did not score.
If he sinks this one, it's curtains for that team.	A player is taking a penalty kick and if he scores it will mean that the opposition will lose the match.
If he thinks he can out-run him, he has another think coming.	A player might think he can stop an opponent by running faster than him, but he will find it very hard to do as the other player is very fast.
If he turns it on today they could win it.	A certain player is very good and if he plays well his team could win the match.
If they beat them, I will eat my hat.	I think a certain team (e.g. Bolton) has no chance of beating another (e.g. Manchester United) and I would be astonished if they did.

Is he going to show up or is he just going to hide in the shadows?	Is a good player going to try to play well and give a hundred percent or is he not going to try?
Is there a hero in the ranks today?	A team could win the game, but someone must score a very good goal.
It crept over the line.	The ball went slowly over the goal-line.
It just fizzled out to a nil-nil draw.	A match started out quite well, but as the game went on, it became very dull and boring and neither side scored.
It looked like his feet were glued to the ground.	A goal-keeper let the ball go past him and did not move to save it.
It looks like a two-horse race now.	It looks like two teams alone are now fighting it out for the league title. They are too far ahead for any other team to catch up with them.
It looks like it's just handbags.*	Two players are arguing, perhaps pushing or slapping each other, but they are not really using their fists.
It should have been all over by half time.	A team should have scored more goals. They should have been well in front (i.e. they should have had many more goals than the other team) by half time.
It takes two to tango.*	Both players are in the wrong.
It took a bad bounce.	A player missed a ball, or could not control it, as it hit an uneven part of the pitch.
It veered off the outside of his foot.	A player was taking a shot and the ball was "sliced" off his foot and missed the target.
It was a one-man show.	One player was playing so well that he won the game for his team.

It was harder to miss.	A player has just missed a very easy chance to score a goal.
It will be very hard to knock them off the top.	A team is on top of the league. It will be very hard to move it from that position by earning more points and taking its place at the top of the league.
It will take a miracle to save them now.	A team is losing very badly, and there's not much chance of their winning the game.
It'll all end in tears.	It isn't going to work out well for them, and people will be upset.
It's a cliff-hanger.	It's a really well-contested game, very close and exciting. Either one of the teams could win.
It's a cut and thrust game.	It's a very good, exciting, fast-paced game.
It's a double-edged sword.	It can be a good thing or a bad thing. / It can be to the advantage of either side.
It's a game of two halves.	A football match can change unexpectedly over the ninety minutes of play, especially between the first and second half of the match.
It's a lot of dough for a young player.	A young player is making a lot of money for his age.
It's a nail-biting finish.	It's a very exciting game, which could go either way.
It's a nerve-wracking five minutes.	The team which is winning the game is trying very hard not to let the other team score and get back into the game; and the supporters of the winning team are very nervous and want the game to end.
It's a toss up.	Either of two possibilities is equally likely.

It's a toss-up between George and Eric for the striker's position.	It's equally likely that either George or Eric may be chosen for the striker's position.
It's all going off now.	The players are losing their tempers and fighting with each other.
It's all gone horribly wrong.	A team which was winning is now playing very badly and losing badly.
It's all gone pear-shaped now.	It's all gone wrong (e.g. they might have been winning but now they're getting beaten).
It's always in the back of his mind.	A player is a bit nervous, for some reason. perhaps he has just come back from a broken leg and is worried about getting hurt again.
It's brass monkey's out there.	It's freezing cold weather in the stadium.
It's come to fisti-cuffs now.	Some players are having a fight with their fists, punching each other.
It's easier said than done.	It's easier to give advice than to implement it.
It's going to be a very cagey game.	Both teams will play very cautiously.
It's in the bag now.	A team should win the game.
It's just not on.	A player shouldn't have done something. It wasn't right to do it.
It's lashing down from the heavens.	It's raining very hard.
It's like a quagmire out there. The players are slipping all over the place.	The pitch is very bad – very muddy – because of the rain or snow.
It's like a war-zone out there.	A game is very unpleasant, nasty and unfair. Many fouls are being

	committed.
It's never over until the fat lady sings.	You should never celebrate a win, until the final whistle goes. The game could change very quickly. It's not over until the final whistle blows.
It's not a foregone conclusion.	It's not inevitable that a particular team will win the match.
It's not for the faint-hearted in that box.	The game is very physical and the defenders of a certain team are very aggressive and strong.
It's pouring down out there.	It's raining very hard.
It's raining cats and dogs out there.	It's raining very hard.
It's raising its ugly head again.	The game is becoming very violent. OR The crowd is being very racist.
It's six of one and half a dozen of the other.	Two players, who are challenging for the ball, are each equally guilty of fouling the other.
It's the same old story with him.	A player keeps doing the same things over and over again. (Maybe he keeps getting sent off for doing these things, too.)
It's the same old story with this team.	A team that might be winning a game always lets the opposition get back into the game.
It's time he called it a day.	A player should give up playing and retire.
It's too little too late now.	A team has just scored a goal and has started to play better, but it's too late. It's nearly full-time. They can't possibly win.
It's turned into a dog-fight now.	A match has become very rough.

It's up for grabs [now].	It's a very exciting game that could be won by either team.
It's very slippy under foot out there.	The pitch is very wet because of the rain. It's very hard for the players to keep their footing and they can fall very easily.
It's very touch and go for him now.	A player might be selected for the team or he might not be selected.
Job done.	A team has just won the match.
keep possession	keeping the ball and preventing the opposing team from getting it
keeps doing something	does something repeatedly
Let's keep our fingers crossed.	Let's wish the team good luck.
like as if (*colloquial*)	as if
lose possession	losing possession of the ball to the other side
Man on!	A shout to warn a team-mate that a player from the other team is right behind him. This is often a call to pass the ball quickly.
My granny could have scored that one.*	A player has just missed a very easy chance to score.
Nine times out of ten he would put that away.	The player would normally score from that position.
No-one wants to slip up now.	No-one wants to make a mistake now.
Not by a country mile.	A team has no chance of winning a certain game.
Now he's had a	A player who might have come from

taste of the big time, he . . .	the lower leagues is now playing in the top league and will not want to go back to a lower league.
nutmeg	A trick or technique in which a player passes the ball through an opponent's legs and then collects it from the other side. (For example: "Rooney nutmegged the Chelsea defender Ashley Cole".)
one-touch football	An often admiring reference to a style of football in which a team can pass the ball quickly from one player to another without the need to control it with more than one touch.
park	pitch, field
right (used as an intensifier) (*colloquial*)	very
score on	scored against
steaming back across the goal	A player has passed the ball across the goal for his team-mate to try to score.
That coach doesn't beat around the bush.	The coach says exactly what he thinks.
That could change the face of the game now.	An incident has happened which could change the outcome of a match. (E.g. one team might be winning and one of their players has been sent off.)
That goal has wiped the smile of his face.	A manager or coach is unhappy because his team was winning but they have now conceded a goal, making the score even. He looked happy before, but now looks very stern.
That goal was a fluke.	The goal a player scored was very lucky; not really a good goal.

That has nil-nil written all over it.	The game looks as if it will be very boring, perhaps because both teams only want a draw.
That has put the dampeners on a good game.	Something has happened to spoil the game. (E.g. someone might have been sent off for fighting.)
That has them rocking and reeling.	A team has just conceded a goal and they are very shocked by this.
That hit him right where it hurts.	The ball has hit the player in the crotch between the legs.
That incident has overshadowed the whole game.	Something bad happened in the match (e.g. someone got a bad injury, or two players started to fight).
That is a very nice stripe they have.	A team has a very colourful football jersey.
That knocked the stuffing out of him.	A player has been hit hard by the ball / was tackled very hard and is suffering from the impact.
That might come back to bite them.	A team should have done something but didn't and they may regret it in future because it may have a bad result.
That miss will haunt him for ever.	A player will never forget a very bad miss as long as he lives.
That one sailed over the top.	The ball was kicked way over the top of the crossbar.
That pass was never on.	The player should not have attempted to pass to his team-mate.
That player / team has a Jekyll and Hyde mentality.	Sometimes a player / team will behave and play very well and next time the player / the team will behave and play very badly.
That shot stung the keeper's palms.	The shot on the goal was so hard that when the goal-keeper stopped it with his hands he must have felt some pain.

That shot was driven home.	The player scored a great goal by kicking the ball hard and successfully.
That shot was right out of the blue.	A player shot at the goal when nobody thought he would.
That should have wrapped it all up by now.	A team who is winning and playing very well should have scored more goals to make sure of the win.
That tackle nearly cut him in half.	A player, challenged for the ball, hit his opponent very hard at waist height. This is very dangerous play and a foul.
That team will just grind them down.	A team will keep running and putting pressure on the other team for most of game and will eventually score.
That was a beauty.	A player has either just scored a great goal or had a great shot at the goal.
That was a big wake-up call for them.	A team which thought it was very good has just been beaten by a poor team.
That was a blinding first half.	The first half of a match was very fast and exciting.
That was a bobby-dazzler.	A player has scored a great goal / just made a great move.
That was a bullet of a header.	A player had a header at the goal with tremendous power.
That was a cavalier performance.	A player has just had a great game.
That was a classic [goal].	A player has just scored a great goal.
That was a clever little ball-in.	A player passed a very good pass into the box to his team-mate.
That was a clinical finish.	A player controlled the ball and hit a well-placed shot past the goal-keeper.
That was a close shave.	A shot just missed the goal by inches.

That was a close-range header.	A player had a chance to score from very close to the goal.
That was a clumsy challenge.	A very late challenge for the ball resulted in a foul.
That was a cracking goal.	That was a very spectacular goal (which has just been scored).
That was a crisp pass.	A player made a very good pass.
That was a darting run.	A player made a very quick run into a good position.
That was a decent effort.	A player had a very good try at scoring but just missed.
That was a desperate challenge.	A player attempted a despairing challenge as a last resort.
That was a ding-dong battle out there.	The match was very exciting; a very good, well-fought, hard-tackling game.
That was a double bubble.	The match that is being played is worth double the points.
That was a double whammy.	Bad luck struck twice on the team / on a player.
That was a driving run into the box.	A player made a very fast run into the box to try a get a goal.
That was a fifty-fifty ball.	Two players went for the same ball and perhaps collided with each other.
That was a free header he got there.	A player jumped and headed the ball and no one from the opposing team challenged him for it.
That was a gem of a ball.	That was a very good shot or pass.
That was a golden opportunity.	A player had an easy chance (e.g. to score in front of the goal), but missed it.

That was a good back-header.	A player (mainly a forward) tried to score or pass using the back of his head.
That was a good change of gear.	A player changed speed very effectively.
That was a good early ball.	A player passed to his team-mate quickly.
That was a good lay-off.	A player made a very good pass.
That was a great searching ball-in.	A player made an excellent long pass to his team-mate.
That was a hospital ball.	A player passed the ball to his team-mate but passed too far in front of him. As a result, an opponent could challenge and the team-mate could suffer an injury. A bad pass.
That was a humdinger.	A player has just scored a good goal or had a real good hard shot at the goal.
That was a lovely weighted pass.	That was a very good pass to a team-mate; not too fast or hard.
That was a nasty dead leg.	A player has suffered a challenge from an opponent's knee that hit him in his thigh and is very painful.
That was a nice little flick-on.	A player headed the ball over the defense for his team-mate to run on to it.
That was a nice little shimmy.	A player has made a good move by swinging his hips and deceiving his opponent.
That was a nice little touch-on.	A player made a good pass to his team-mate by just touching the ball on to him with a part of his body (e.g. with his head, foot, knee, or heel).
That was a pearler.	That was a very good shot or pass.

That was a piece of magic.	A player performed some brilliant technique on the ball or scored a brilliant goal.
That was a pin-point header.	That was a very accurate header. – A player has just made a very good header at the goal and scored.
That was a point-blank save.	The goal-keeper saved the ball from right in front of him.
That was a poor delivery.	That was a bad pass. (It might have conceded a corner.)
That was a real upset.	A team has won the match against all the odds.
That was a really harsh decision.	The referee gave a foul but the action that led to the decision didn't look that bad.
That was a right drubbing.	A team has just been beaten very badly.
That was a right let-off.	A team has conceded a goal, but the referee disallowed it.
That was a right walk-over.	A team has just been beaten very badly by many goals, say 4-0, or 5-0.
That was a robust challenge.	That was a very strong clumsy tackle.
That was a rocket.	A player has just hit a very hard powerful shot.
That was a school-boy error.	A professional player has made a very basic mistake, which he should not have made.
That was a scorcher.	A player has just scored a very good goal with tremendous power.
That was a scrappy game.	It wasn't a very good game. Not much skill was used.
That was a screamer.	A very good goal has just been scored. It was spectacular!

That was a short-lived lead.	A team, which took the lead early in the game, has just conceded a goal, and the score is now even.
That was a soft goal to let in.	The goal-keeper let a very easy shot get past him.
That was a spanking goal.	A player has just scored a great goal.
That was a split-second decision.	The referee made his decision very quickly. / A player had no time to think and had to act very fast.
That was a sucker punch.	A team that might have been winning or might have been playing their best has just conceded a goal.
That was a telling ball.	That was a very good long pass to a team-mate.
That was a toe poke.	The player used his toe to score or pass the ball.
That was a top-drawer performance.	A team or player has played very well.
That was a turn up for the book.	A team has won a game they weren't expected to win.
That was a two-footed tackle.	A player slid in towards an opponent with two feet up in the air. (This is very dangerous.)
That was a walk in the park.	That was an easy win for a team.
That was an absolute belter.	A player has just scored a very good goal.
That was an electrifying run.	A player has just made a very fast, exciting run towards his opponents' goal.
That was an outstanding	A team or a player has just had a brilliant game.

performance.

That was below the belt, that one.	That was unfair. (E.g. a player made a very bad tackle on a player, OR a coach has made a bad comment about someone.)
That was brilliant foot-work.	A player has just made some brilliant moves (e.g. dribbling or turning).
That was just a whisker away.	A shot at the goal just missed by a few inches.
That was part and parcel of his game.	That's the way this player always plays. It's his style of play.
That was their last-ditch effort.	A team is putting its all into the last few minutes of the game, to try to save or win a match.
That was top-drawer.	A player has just made a play (a shot or pass) that was brilliant.
That was very risky.	A player is trying to pass the ball or dribble with it in a dangerous area of the football pitch, and this could lead to his team conceding a goal.
That was very sloppy play.	A team keeps giving the ball away and is playing very badly.
That wasn't much to write home about.	That was a very boring game; not good to watch.
That will put his name up in lights now.	A player has just scored a great goal / had a tremendous game.
That would have knocked him into the middle of next week.	A shot was hit so hard, that if a player had got in the way of it, it would have hurt him very badly.
That would have knocked his lights out.	A player has taken a very hard shot and if the opposing player had got in front of it, he would have been injured or

	knocked unconscious.
That wraps up the points for them now.	The team has secured the points that it needs for a particular objective.
That's a dream start for them.	A team has scored a goal very early in the game.
That's a good scalp to take.	A team has just beaten a team that is higher than them in the league.
That's a mis-match.	A player who is very good is up against a player who is not so good. / One team is at a very much higher level than the other.
That's given them a new lease of life now.	A team has just scored a goal and is now starting to play better.
That's gone begging.	That was a missed chance to score.
That's his bogey team.	The team he's playing against is not very lucky for him, and he never wins against them.
That's his first goal for his boyhood club.	A player has just scored a goal for the team he supported as a boy.
That's part and parcel of his armour.	The way the player plays the game is his very own style.
That's put the last nail in the coffin.	A team might be winning very easily and has just scored perhaps in the last minute, so there's no chance for the other team.
That's the ace in his pack.	A coach has a very good player, whom he hopes is going to win the game for him.
The ball bobbled over the line.	The ball bounced and moved slowly over the line.

The ball was stolen from him that time.	A player has just had the ball taken from him very easily.
The bubble's burst now.	A team which was on a winning streak has just been badly beaten.
The coach doesn't mince words.	The coach says exactly what he thinks.
The coach is giving them a right tongue-lashing.	The coach or manager is very upset with his team and is giving them a very stern talking-to (i.e. substantial criticism).
The coach is screaming from the line.	The coach of a team is shouting orders to his team.
The coach is straight to the point.	The coach says exactly what he thinks.
The compliment has been returned.	A player might have made a goal from his team-mate, and now his team-mate has just done the same for him.
The crowd is always on his back.	The crowd is always criticizing him loudly.
the deck	the field / ground / pitch
The defender keeps diving in.	The defender makes a challenge for the ball too quickly and lets the forward go past him.
The drop seems inevitable now.	A team which is at the bottom of the league looks like going down to a lower league.
The element of surprise caught him.	A player was caught unaware and was beaten by a pass. / The keeper conceded a goal.
the flight of the ball	the way the ball is coming towards a player in the air
The game has died	A match has become very boring

59

a death now.	without much action.
The game's in its death throes now.	The game looks like it's over and a certain team will lose.
The game's out of reach now.	One team is well in front and the other team will not catch them.
The goal-keeper made a howler.	The goal-keeper made a very basic mistake and caused a goal to be scored past him.
The home supporters keep getting on his back.	A player is getting a lot of abuse and name-calling from the supporters.
The keeper had a right nightmare.	The goal-keeper had a very bad game.
The keeper has butter-fingers.	The goal-keeper keeps letting the ball slip out of his hands.
The keeper is quick off his line.	The goal-keeper is fast and makes quick decisions as to when to leave the goal in order to prevent an attacking player from scoring past him.
The keeper launched it up-field.	The goal-keeper kicked the ball very hard towards the opposition's goal.
The manager has given him a free roll.	The manager told the player he can go anywhere on the field. He doesn't have to stay in one position.
The manager has got the chop / got the axe / got the sack / been fired.	The manager has lost his job.
The manager will be over the moon with that win.	The manager will be very happy that his team has won the match.
The manager's playing mind games.	The manager of a team is not being straight with the other manager (e.g. he's saying things about the

	opposition).
The pitch is heavy on the legs. / It's heavy-going.	The pitch is very bad, because of rain or snow. The resulting mud is making it very hard to run and the players' legs are getting very tired.
The pitch looks like a ploughed field.	Because of the rain or snow the pitch looks in very bad shape, all bumpy and uneven.
The referee keeps waving him away.	A player, who disagrees with the referee's decisions and keeps running up to him, is consistently waved away by the referee.
The referee needs to nip that in the bud.	A player might be committing some bad fouls and the referee needs to talk to him.
The referee won't stand for any of that nonsense.	The referee is a very good referee and will discipline a player if he keeps misbehaving.
The referee's got it in for him. He keeps picking on him.	The referee keeps cautioning a certain player during the game.
The referee's on top of this game.	The referee is having a good game.
The right full-back keeps back-peddling.	A defender keeps moving back as the forward comes at him.
the six-yard box	the goal-keeper's box
the stats	the statistics of the game (i.e., how many goals, corners, passes, fouls, etc. have been scored / taken place)
The tackles are flying in now thick and fast.	The game is very competitive and both teams are tackling very hard to win the ball.
The team has a	The team's defense is very strong and

solid defence.	dependable.
The team is running out of steam.	The players are getting very tired.
The team needs to play the big man little man scenario.	A team needs to have a large, tall, strong player alongside a fast, small player, to play as a partnership and try to score.
The team's doing very poorly.	A team's losing a lot of games.
The tempo has dropped now.	A match that started very fast has slowed down considerably.
The travelling hordes are in raptures.	The supporters of an away team are very loud or singing as their team has just won or scored a goal.
the way they are setting out their stall	the way the coach is planning his formation for the match
the way this game's panning out	the way this game's developing
the woodwork	the crossbar / the goal
the worst-case scenario	An example of "the worst-case scenario" is when a player has to play in a different position because one of his team-mates has been injured.
The young players look up to him.	They respect him, because he's senior to them and/or a very good professional.
There are some chinks missing in their armour.	A team isn't playing very well and is being exposed in many positions. Some of their best players may not be playing.
There have them on the back foot.	One team is getting the better of the other team.

There was venom in that shot.	A player hit a very hard shot. It was going very fast.
There's a lot of history between those two.	Two players might not like each other.
There's a lot riding on this game.	Both teams might need the points. It's a very important game.
There's never a dull moment with him.	He's a controversial player who's always getting in trouble, or always doing something out of the ordinary.
There's never a dull moment with that player.	There's always something happening when that player plays.
There's no daylight between them.	A good defender has marked his opposing player very tightly.
There's no love lost between those two players.	The two players don't like each other.
There's no show without punch.	A game has to have excitement to be interesting to watch.
There's no team-spirit there.	A team is not playing well. They aren't trying very hard to support each other.
There's not much in it. It could go either way.	The teams are very evenly matched and either of them could win the game.
There's only one thing in his mind when he gets in front of the goal.	When this player gets in front of the goal, he just wants to shoot and score a goal.
There's some argy-bargy going on in the box.	Some players are pushing each other and being very physical.
These fans will warm to him.	The fans will give him a good reception and will like him.

They are always getting on his case.	The crowd keeps shouting at him or moaning at (i.e. complaining about) him.
They are dangerous on the counter-attack.	A team can switch quickly from defense to attack, and score in that way.
They are dominating in the air.	A team is very powerful at heading the ball and wins many challenges / duels from high balls.
They are giving the ball away too cheaply.	The players keep losing possession of the ball too easily.
They are having a little tussle in mid-field.	Two players are pushing and shoving each other to get control of the ball.
They are playing route-one football.	A team is playing a long ball game over the defense with long high passes.
They are strong in the air.	A team has a lot of tall players who can head the ball very well.
They are the giant-killers of the cup.	A team from the lower leagues has beaten a team from a higher league (e.g. a Liverpool professional club from the premier league has been beaten by semi-professionals from a lower league).
They are turning things around now.	A team that was getting beaten is starting to play better and now has a chance to win the game.
They batted them.	One team won convincingly, by many goals.
They blitzed the opposition.	They won very easily.
They blow hot and cold sometimes.	A team sometimes plays well, sometimes badly.

They can fill their boots now.	A team which is winning very easily should score / should have a chance to score many goals.
They can see the light at the end of the tunnel.	A team is doing well and if they keep playing well they could win the game.
They can still put themselves in the mix.	A team is still in the running (i.e. still has a chance) to win the league.
They clawed their way back into the game.	A team which has been getting beaten for most of the game is now turning things around and starting to play better.
They don't have the strength or depth.	A team does not have a strong squad of quality players. / They have a small squad.
They got a luke-warm reception from the crowd.	A certain team did not receive much applause even from their supporters.
They got a right mauling.	A team was beaten very badly.
They got stuck in!	A team has a lot of determination and fought very hard to try and win the game
They had a bad drubbing.	A team was thoroughly beaten.
They had a bit of a blip.	A team which was doing well has started to have a drop in form (i.e. to play less well).
They hammered them.	A team has just beaten another team very badly, e.g. 5-0.
They have a bus-load of talent.	A team has many very good quality players.
They have a dodgy defense.	A team has a very bad defense.

They have a right mountain to climb now.	A team is getting beaten very badly.
They have an up-hill battle now.	A team is being beaten and will find it very hard to get back into the game.
They have been rock-solid so far.	A team has been very good and the defense is very strong.
They have cemented themselves to the top of the league.	A team is well out in front, at the top of the division, and is likely to remain there.
They have got to put them out of their misery.	A team which is winning easily neds to finish the other side off by scoring again.
They have had a slight dip in form lately.	The team's form has slipped and it isn't performing up to its usual standard of play.
They have started very slowly	A team isn't playing very well.
They have stepped up the pace of the game.	A team has started to run and move much more quickly as the game progresses.
They have taken their foot off the pedal now.	A team which was in charge and winning easily has now slowed the pace of the game and is not so dominant.
They have the edge now.	A team looks as though it will win the match.
They have their tails in the air now.	A team which is winning looks very confident and the players are enjoying the game.
They have them on the back foot now.	A certain team is putting considerable pressure on the opposing team and is on top of the game (i.e. in control).
They have thrown	A team has made a determined

down the gauntlet.	challenge to win.
They have to be careful that the trickle does not become a flood.	A team which is presently losing by only one or two goals has to be careful that they don't lose by five or six.
They have to clear their lines.	A team must defend better by getting out of the box altogether.
They have to make something happen early doors.	A team needs to score early on in the game to stand a good chance of winning.
They have to step it up a notch. / They have to step it up soon.	A team must work harder to try to win the game.
They have to take the game to them.	The team must attack the other team.
They haven't a hope in hell's chance.	A particular team (perhaps they are in a lower league) has no chance whatever to win the game.
They haven't a hope.	The team doesn't have any chance of winning.
They haven't given up the ghost yet.	A team which is getting beaten in a game is still trying its best to win. OR A team is still trying to become top of the league. At the moment, they might be in second position, but they won't give up the attempt to be first.
They haven't seen a lot of the ball.	A team hasn't been in control of the ball very much.
They hit the woodwork.	A team kicked the ball against the goal crossbar or against a goal post.
They keep acting as if the ball is a hot potato.	A team keeps losing the ball.
They keep	Two players are trying to get control of

grappling away at each other.	the ball.
They keep packing the midfield.	A team keeps putting many players in the middle of the field to stop the other team getting through.
They keep playing the ball high into the danger area.	A team is kicking the ball high into the goal-keeper's box.
They keep playing the offside trap.	A team's defense keeps trying to catch the forwards offside by moving out quickly.
They keep playing with the lone striker.	A team always plays with only one forward.
They keep putting square pegs in round holes.	The balance of a team is continually upset by playing players in positions where they don't usually play and where they don't perform well.
They keep trying to wind him up.	Some players on a team keep trying to make a certain player lose his composure or temper by saying unpleasant things to him.
They keep using bullying tactics.	A team is playing very roughly to put the other team off their game: for example, they are pushing and shoving.
They look like they're in the comfort zone.	A team is safe from relegation (i.e. from being moved down to a lower division).
They lost it by the odd goal.	A team just lost the match by one goal. (E.g. Newcastle 1 Liverpool 0.)
They missed too many easy chances.	A team has not played well and missed many goal-scoring chances.
They must have been working on	A team has just scored a very good goal or attempted to score with a free

that set piece in training.	kick.
They need a big man up there.	A team needs a big strong player in the forward line.
They need a good run in the cup.	A team needs to play well and win some games in a cup competition.
They need a little bit of steel in their defense.	A team's defense is a little soft and it needs to be more aggressive.
They need that elusive away win.	A team must win an away game soon.
They need to brush up on their passing.	A team is not very good at passing the ball and must work at it in training.
They need to come up with the goods.	A team which is supposed to be good needs to prove they are good by playing well and scoring some goals.
They need to go back to the basics.	The players in a team which has been beaten and/or made some very basic mistakes need to refresh themselves, perhaps in their training sessions.
They need to hit the back of the net more.	A team is not scoring many goals and they need to do so.
They need to keep it nice and tight now.	The team which is winning the game needs to get their defence to mark the opposition players very closely.
They need to keep the ball on the deck.	The team needs to pass the ball along the ground and not keep playing high balls.
They need to pick up their game.	A team needs to start playing better, to try to win the game.
They need to put this side to the sword.	One team is much better and is winning the game easily; but they must get some more goals to make sure they do win and thus finish off the game.

They need to slow the game down.	A team has to pass the ball more slowly.
They need to stand up and be counted.	Some players are not trying very hard and/or aren't playing very well. They need to start playing better.
They need to stay in the top flight.	A team needs to stay in the premier league, and not be relegated down to a lower league.
They need to stop the rot.	A team is, for example, losing too many games and needs to start winning some.
They play with lovely rhythm.	A team is very good and makes everything look very easy with good passing and movement.
They put eleven men behind the ball.	A team defended with all the players. It wasn't very interested in scoring goals but was happy with a draw.
They ran the defense ragged.	The forwards made the defense work very hard and made the defenders look very uncomfortable.
They scrambled the ball over the line.	Some players forced the ball over the goal line, to score what was not a very pretty goal but a goal all the same.
They sent this team home packing.	A team has just won at home very well.
They share the spoils.	Both teams share the points. / The game was a draw: e.g. 0-0, 1-1, etc.
They should have put the game to bed.	A team which was well in front should have scored more goals and finished the other team off.
They should not get carried away.	The team that is winning should not become too confident.
They shouldn't count their chickens.	A team shouldn't think they have won until the final whistle.

They think he's the bee's knees up [in] that part of the world.	The supporters of a team love and respect a certain player who plays for them.
They were all over them like a rash.	A team had the ball and the opposition was very quick to close them down and tackle for the ball.
They were badly drubbed.	A team was thoroughly beaten.
They were caught by a sucker punch that time.	A team which was dominating most of the game conceded a goal against the run of play.
They were caught flat-footed.	A team conceded a goal by losing concentration.
They were pipped at the post.	A team conceded a goal right at the end of the match – maybe 1-0 – in the last seconds.
They were robbed.	A defeat was unjust. The referee robbed them of a win with a particular decision that he gave.
They were soaking up all the pressure and they caught them on the break.	One team which was defending for most of the game broke away and scored a goal.
They were turned over big time.	A team got beaten very badly by many goals.
They will fight tooth and nail for it.	A team will give their best to try to win the game and will never give up trying.
They will tear them apart.	One team will win the game very easily.
They won it hands down.	A team won the match very easily.
They won't go with a fancy-dan shape.	A team won't change its normal line-up to something showy (which perhaps

	they've never tried).
They won't let them settle.	One team will chase and challenge very strongly, so as not to let the other team get control of the game.
They're all at sixes and sevens.	A team is playing very badly and nothing is going right for them.
They're all over the place.	A team's players are not playing very well and they are all out of position.
They're all over them now.	A team is playing very well and has most of the play.
They're all scurrying forward.	Many players are moving forward at the same time.
They're back in with a shout.	A team that was getting beaten has just scored and now has a chance of winning the game. OR A team is catching up with the league leaders.
They're cruising now.	A team is winning very easily.
They're facing very obtuse opposition.	A team is playing against a very stubborn and determined opposition.
They're flushed with success.	A team is very happy and euphoric at winning many games.
They're getting too big for their boots.	A team thinks they are so good they can't be beaten.
They're hanging on by the skin of their teeth.	They're just managing to avoid being beaten / to keep their lead.
They're in the driving seat now.	A team is winning very easily and controlling the game. They're on top of their game and should win.
They're looking for more silverware.	A team is trying to win the league and trophies.
They're not firing on all cylinders.	A team which normally plays well is not performing up to its own standard.

They're off the mark.	A team is in the lead, having scored a goal first.
They're on a hiding to nothing.	A team, which is going to play against a very strong team – perhaps from a higher division – will have no chance of winning and will be beaten very badly.
They're on fire right now.	A team is playing very well and is winning games.
They're playing like a bunch of doughnuts.	A team is playing very badly.
They're playing like a bunch of old women.	The players are playing very badly as a team and are very slow.
They're playing too square at the back.	A team is not defending very well and is playing too straight at the back of the defense and this will let the other team score.
They're playing with a good deal of swagger.	A team is playing very well and looks as if it is in total control.
They're riding their luck.	A team that is winning a game is doing risky things that could make them lose or concede a goal or goals.
They're ripping them apart now.	A team is winning very easily.
They're running riot now.	A team has really beaten another team very badly, say by 4-0 or 5-0.
They're soaking up the pressure now.	A team is defending well.
They're steaming forward now.	A team is attacking the goal in force.
They're still a man to the good.	A team has all their players still on the field, while their opponents have had

one player sent off.

They're still looking for that elusive first goal.	A team might not have scored for a while and the players are trying hard / hoping to get a goal soon.
They're trying to cheat the referee	A team is trying to break the rules without the referee noticing.
They're up against it big time now.	A team is having a very hard time and is getting beaten.
They've got bigger fish to fry.	A team is not worried about a certain opposing team, which they think they can beat easily. Instead they are concerned about a better team which they need to beat.
They've had two defeats on the trot.	A team has lost two matches in a row.
They've hit rock bottom now.	A team is now at the bottom of the League and playing very badly.
They've just been giving a lesson on how to pass the ball.	A team has just played very well and their passing has been very good; a model for others to follow.
This could be the last throw of the dice.	A team which is losing is making a last attempt at trying to win the game (for example, by bringing on a substitute).
This game is end to end.	The game is very exciting and each team is attacking each other's goal.
This game should be in the bag now.	A team that is winning will probably not lose the game now.
This game will be no cake-walk.	A team which thinks it might be easy to win the game will be in for a shock, as it will be harder than they expect.
This is edge-of-the-seat stuff now.	A match is becoming very exciting with a great deal of action.
This is going down	A match is very even and could be won

to the wire.	by either side at the very last minute of the game.
This is going right to the death.	A match is very even and could be tied right up to the last minute and someone might still win it in the last minute.
This is good, flowing football.	The match is being played very well and is good to watch.
This is not a pretty game.	A match has very hard tackling and not very much skill is being used.
This is still wide open.	The match is very even and either side could win it.
This player is a diamond in the rough / a little rough round the edges.	A new young player will, in the future, be a very good player, after he gets more experience and learns the game more.
This player needs no introduction.	He's a fantastic player. Everyone knows who he is.
This team has a mountain to climb now.	A team which is losing the game by a few goals doesn't have much chance.
This team has to dig deep.	The team must try much harder if they want to win the game.
This team has turned the corner.	A team which was playing badly is starting to play better, and winning some games.
This team is flexing their muscles now.	A team is very strong and starting to take control of the game.
This team is running out of steam.	The players are becoming very tired.
This team needs to pull their socks up.	A team is not playing very well.

This team will bounce back.	Although a team has been beaten, it will recover from the loss and could win the next game.
This team will struggle in this league.	A team will never win many games in its present league and it could be relegated to a lower league.
This team's at sixes and sevens.	A team is not playing well, is unsure and confused.
This team's dead and buried now.	A team is getting beaten very badly and has no chance of winning the match.
This team's got lovely shape to it.	A team is looking very good and well-organized.
This team's not gelling together.	A team's not playing well / not playing well as a unit.
This time he would not be denied.	A player who previously had a chance to score, but was stopped by a player or by the goal-keeper, had another chance. This time he scored.
This will go down to the wire.	The match is very close and either team could win it at the end of the ninety minutes.
to send the keeper the wrong way	A player can fool the goal-keeper and pretend to shoot at one side of the goal while the ball goes in another direction. (This expression is often used when penalties are taken.)
to switch play	To change the direction of the play and pass the ball from one side of the pitch to the other. (E.g. "He switched play from the left to the right wing.")
We just weren't at the races today.	A team just did not play the way they normally do.
We never turned up for it.	We didn't perform as we should have done (*A coach may say this, talking*

	about his team which has just been beaten.)
What a clumsy challenge that was!	That was a very bad mis-timed tackle.
What a crunching tackle that was! / That was a cruncher!	A player made a very strong challenge for the ball, perhaps injuring the player he tackled.
What a fantastic strike!	A player has just had a great shot at the goal / scored a very good goal.
You can feel the gathering gloom around the stadium.	A team might be in a bad position in the league and could be relegated. The fans can feel this, so the mood of the fans in the stadium is not a happy one.
You can't let them get into their stride.	If one team lets the other team control the speed and tempo of the game, they will lose the match.
You don't need to be a rocket scientist to know he should have done better.	A coach is talking about a player who should have played better and everyone knows it.
You don't see many of those per dozen.	A player has done something spectacular. You don't see that level of skill very often.
You don't want to rub him up the wrong way.	You don't want to upset him.
You have to put a man on him all the game.	A certain player is very good. To stop him from playing well, a team has to arrange for one of their players to mark him very tightly all through the match.

* Please see the Table of Illustrations for the page reference to where some of these sayings are illustrated.

He looks like he has two left feet.

He needs to wake up and smell the roses.

He seems to have his head in the clouds.

He's on fire today.

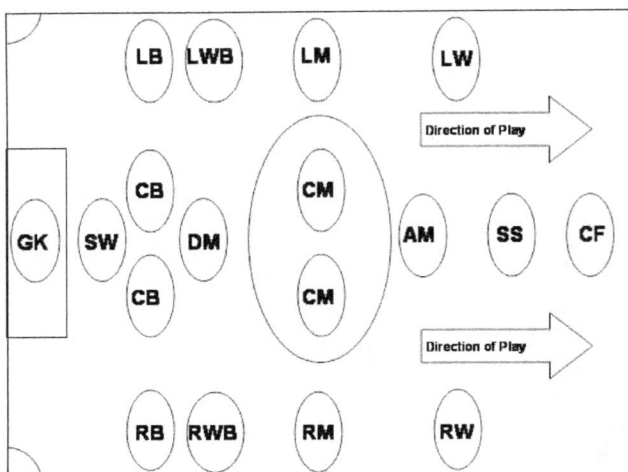

The diagram shows football positions on a pitch:

LB | LWB | LM | LW

Direction of Play →

CB | CM

GK | SW | DM | AM | SS | CF

CB | CM

Direction of Play →

RB | RWB | RM | RW

Football positions

Please note: There are only eleven players in a team! The above diagram shows the different places where players may be assigned and the different names given to various playing positions from time to time.

Football positions

Each of the eleven players in a team is assigned to a particular position on the field of play. They include a goalkeeper and ten outfield players who fill various defensive, midfield and attacking positions depending on the formation deployed. The following lists all the positions, together with the abbreviations commonly used. Please note that the Centre Forward can be interchanged with a Striker.

- 1 Goalkeeper (GK)
- 2 Defensive positions
    - 2.1 Centre-back (CB)
    - 2.2 Sweeper/Libero (SW)
    - 2.3 Full-back (FB/RB/LB)
    - 2.4 Wingback (WB/RWB/LWB)
- 3 Midfield positions
    - 3.1 Centre midfield (CM)
    - 3.2 Defensive midfielder (DM)
    - 3.3 Attacking midfielder (AM)
    - 3.4 Side midfielders (LM/RM)
    - 3.5 Winger (RW/LW)
- 4 Strikers/forwards
    - 4.1 Centre forward (CF)
    - 4.2 Striker (S)
    - 4.3 Deep-lying forwards (SS)

These positions describe both the main role of each player and his area of operation on the pitch. However, the fluid nature of the modern football game means that the positions are not as formally defined as in rugby and American football, for example. As the game has evolved, tactics and team formations have changed, and the names of the positions and the duties involved have evolved as well. The diagram shows the various positions on the field (diagram not to scale).

He's turned out to be a right lemon.

He's walking a tightrope out there.

Basic football vocabulary

Vocabulary	Explanation
Attack	To make a forceful attempt to score a goal.
Attacker	A player who has possession of the ball.
Away game	When a team plays on a ground other than its own.
Away team	The team that is visiting their opponents' ground.
Ball	An air-filled sphere, which players kick in football. It has the following specifications: a circumference of 68–70 cm (or 27–28 inches), a weight of 410–450 g (or 14–16 ounces), inflated to a pressure of 60–110 kPa (or 8.5–15.6 psi), and covered in leather or "other suitable material".
Beat	To defeat.
Bench	A long seat for several people.
Captain	A player who leads and directs the other players on the football pitch.
Centre circle	A circular marking in the centre of the football pitch, from which the kick-offs are taken.
Centre line	A line that runs across the centre of the field; the halfway line; midfield line.
Champions	A team that has beaten all the other teams in the league or other sporting contest.
Changing-rooms	The rooms where players dress to play.
Cheer	To shout encouragement and to give support.
Coach	A person who trains a team.
Corner kick	A restart of the game, where the ball is kicked from one of the four corners of the pitch.
Cross	A pass from an attacking player near the

	sideline to a team player in the middle, or on the opposite side, of the field. A ball hit across the pitch.
Crossbar	The horizontal beam across the top of the goal.
Defend	To resist an attack.
Defenders	The players who do not have possession of the ball.
Draw / Tie (*noun*)	A game where each team has the same number of goals at the end, or where neither team has scored any goals at all.
Dropped ball	A way of restarting the game, where the referee drops the ball between two players.
Equalizer	A goal that makes the score even (i.e. the same for both teams).
Extra time	A further period of play added on to the game if the scores are equal.
Field	The rectangular, grassed area where a game is played; the pitch.
Field markings	The straight and curved white lines painted onto the field.
FIFA	Fédération Internationale de Football Association.
FIFA world cup	A solid gold statue given to the champions of each World Cup tournament to keep for the next four years.
First half	The first forty-five minutes of the game before half-time.
Fit	In form; in good health.
Fixture	A game played on a particular date.
Fixture list	A programme of games.
Forward	One of the three or four players on a team who is responsible for most of the scoring.
Foul	An unfair or invalid piece of play against the rules.
Free kick	A kick is given to a player for a foul by the opposition. The player kicks the ball

	without any opposing players within ten yards of him.
Friendly game	A game that is not part of a serious contest.
Goal	1) A ball that crosses the goal line between the goal posts and below the crossbar. 2) The structure consisting of two posts, linked by a crossbar, into which all the goals are scored,
Goal area	The rectangular area twenty yards wide by six yards deep in front of each goal.
Goal kick	A way of restarting the game, where the ball is kicked from the inside of the goal area, away from the goal.
Goal line	The boundary or line at each end of the field.
Goal scorer	A player who puts the ball into the goal and so scores a goal.
Goalkeeper / Goalie	The player in front of the goal, who tries – with his hands or body – to stop the other team scoring.
Goalpost	One of the two upright posts of a goal, each eight feet in height.
Ground	The place where a game is played.
Half-time	The fifteen-minute rest period between the first half and second half of a game.
Hand ball	A foul, when a player touches the ball with his arm or hand.
Header	When a player strikes the ball with his head.
Home	A team's own ground.
Hooligan	A violent troublemaker.
Injured player	A player who has been hurt or wounded.
Injury	Physical damage suffered by a player (e.g. a broken leg or a sprained ankle).
Injury time	Time added to the end of the first or second half of a game, to compensate for time lost

	because of player-injuries.
Keeper	*See "Goal-keeper".*
Kick	To strike or hit the ball with the foot.
Kick off	The start of the game or restart after a goal, when a player kicks the ball forward.
Laws of the game	The seventeen main rules for football, established by FIFA.
League	A group of teams which play each other in competition.
Linesman (one of two assistants to the referee)	The two officials who help the referee. They watch the sidelines, goal lines and offside.
Mark	To keep close to another player, so as to prevent him succeeding against the marker's team.
Match	A game of football.
Midfield	A region of the field near the midfield line.
Midfield line	A line that runs across the centre of the field; centre line; the halfway line.
Midfield players	The players that play behind players playing in forward positions.
National team	The team representing a particular country or nation.
Net	1) A mesh of cord hung over and behind the goal. 2) The goal itself.
Offside	A Law in Association Football which effectively limits how far forward attacking players may be when involved in play.
Opposing team	A team playing against another team.
Own goal	A mistake, when a player kicks the ball inside his own goal. The goal is then awarded to the opposing team.
Pass	When a player kicks the ball to a team-mate.
Penalty area	A rectangular area in front of the goal, forty-four yards wide by eighteen yards

	deep. Also called "the goalkeeper's box".
Penalty kick, penalty shot, spot kick.	A kick from the penalty spot (*see below*) by a player against the opposing goalkeeper for (a) the most serious violations of the rules or (b) in the event of a draw.
Penalty spot	A small circle twelve yards in front of the goal.
Pitch	The area where footballers play a match (the football field).
Possession	Control of the ball.
Red card	A small card, red in colour, which the referee holds up to show that a player must leave the game for very bad behaviour.
Referee (Ref.)	The chief official. He starts and stops the play, makes all the decisions about the rules, and acts as the time-keeper.
Score (*noun*)	The number of goals each team has scored.
Score (*verb*)	To put the ball into the goal to gain a point.
Score a hat trick	When one player scores three goals in the same game. (A perfect hat trick is when a player scores one goal with his right foot, one goal with his left foot, and one goal with his head.)
Scoreboard	Large panel or other display that shows the current score or number of goals for each side.
Scorer	A player who scores or gets a goal.
Second half	The second forty-five minutes of the game. / The part of the game which takes place after half-time.
Send a player off	When a referee tells a player to leave the field for bad behaviour.
Side	One of the two teams playing a game.
Sideline	The line that runs along the length of the field on each side.
Spectator	A person who watches a game in a

	stadium.
Stadium	A special sports ground where football is played, with seats for spectators.
Striker	A player who plays forward and whose job it is to get the goals for his team.
Studs	Small points underneath players' boots, to help prevent players from slipping.
Substitute	A player who replaces another player on the field.
Supporter	A spectator who watches and supports one of the teams and wants that team to win.
Tackle	To try to take the ball away from another player, by kicking or stopping it with the feet.
Team	The members of one side. (Each of the two competing sides has eleven players.)
The halfway line	A line that runs across the centre of the field; centre line.
Ticket tout	A person who tries to sell tickets at a price higher than the official price.
Tie / Draw (*noun*)	When two teams have scored the same number of goals in a game (a draw).
Tiebreaker	The way of choosing the winner of a game when both teams have the same number of goals.
To keep goal	To be the goalkeeper or goalie.
To score a goal	To put the ball into the net or goal.
To shoot at goal	To kick the ball towards the goal.
Touch-line / sideline	The line that runs along the length of the field on each of the four sides.
Underdog	A team that is not expected to win.
Unsporting behaviour	Rude or bad conduct.
Whistle	The instrument that the referee blows to create a loud high-pitched sound (for fouls, kick offs, full times, and half times).

Winger	A forward who plays to the side of the striker.
World Cup	The international football competition, between all the football nations of the world. It is organized by FIFA every four years.
Yellow card	A small card, yellow in colour, which the referee holds up to warn a player for bad behaviour.

My granny could have scored that one.

He's a wily old fox.

He's just switched off now.

He's spat out the dummy now.

It looks like it's just handbags.

Index to key words: Sayings

If , when listening to a commentary, you have heard a word with which you are unfamiliar, look for it in the index that follows. Then check the saying or sayings in which it appears, for the meaning.

94

About the Author[i]

Tommy Martin was born in Newcastle-upon-Tyne in 1956. His love of football started at a very early age, playing in the back lanes of Newcastle, where many young boys learned their skills. Even the poorest, who had no ball, would kick around stones or cans. But if a ball was accidentally kicked into someone's yard, the boy who owned it would knock on the door and say, "Please Mister, can we have our ball back?" Sometimes the impatient reply would be, "If that ball comes in here once more I'll put a knife though it!"

All the boys dreamt of playing for their adored Newcastle United. But the reality was that most of them went to work in the ship-yards or coal mines.

Tommy Martin's dream was to play football at any level, even if he had to leave the Newcastle he loved. "I have been very lucky in my life to have travelled the world doing something I love with a passion, playing for twenty years and now teaching and coaching children football for another twenty years."

At twelve years old he started playing for Walker Boys' Youth Scheme and then for the well-respected Wallsend Boys' Youth Football Club, which developed such world-class players as Peter Beardsley and the great Alan Shearer. Graduating through their youth schemes, Tommy Martin went on to play top class football in the northern leagues of Newcastle. But in 1980 he decided he wanted to travel the world and moved on to Jersey, Israel, Australia, and the USA.

From 1986 to 1994, he played in the California Southern League for the Los Angeles Exiles Football Club, before being recruited by the former Liverpool and England player and coach Jimmy Melia, to join him as a player and skills coach for the Dallas Inter Football Club, where

---

[i] Information supplied courtesy of the Author.

Tommy achieved considerable success with the Club's youth teams.

Tommy's reputation as a skills coach led him, in 1995, to be hired by the USA Olympic Youth Development Program representing the State of Texas, and in 1996, he was voted one of the top skills coaches for the under-thirteen age group by the Southern Youth Coaches Committee of the USA. In 1999/2000 he worked as a skills coach for the Hawaii Youth Soccer Federation in Honolulu and in 2001 he started his own football academy in Palm Beach, Florida, USA, which he ran until 2003. He is now a Physical Education Teacher and Football Coach in Asia, where he also runs his own football skills academies in various schools and is involved with the local professional team where he lives.

Tommy Martin is a fully qualified coach with certified licenses from the English Football Association and FIFA. He holds the American Soccer Federation A licence and also has a certificate in sports management and sports injuries. In 1998 he acquired his teacher's degree in Physical Education from Hartford University, Minnesota, USA.

A top skills coach, he has consistently developed young players from recreation league standard to classic league standard. Many have gone on to win soccer scholarships.

Tommy is the author of the successful football skills book, *Soccer the Right Technique* (USA, 1994).

Tommy Martin is happy to visit schools anywhere in Asia. For information about how to arrange a school visit and to find out about Tommy's football academies in Thailand please contact Tommy through Proverse Hong Kong at <proverse@netvigator.com>.

FIND OUT MORE ABOUT PROVERSE AUTHORS, BOOKS, EVENTS AND LITERARY PRIZES

Visit our website: http://www.proversepublishing.com

Visit our distributor's website: <www.chineseupress.com>

Follow us on Twitter
Follow news and conversation: twitter.com/Proversebooks>
OR
Copy and paste the following to your browser window and follow the instructions: https://twitter.com/#!/ProverseBooks

"Like" us on www.facebook.com/ProversePress

Request our free E-Newsletter
Send your request to info@proversepublishing.com.

Availability
Most titles are available in Hong Kong and world-wide from our Hong Kong based Distributor, The Chinese University of Hong Kong Press, The Chinese University of Hong Kong, Shatin, NT, Hong Kong SAR, China.
Email: cup-bus@cuhk.edu.hk
Website: <www.chineseupress.com>.

All titles are available from Proverse Hong Kong, http://www.proversepublishing.com and the Proverse Hong Kong UK-based Distributor.

Stock-holding retailers
Hong Kong (Growhouse, Bookazine)
Singapore (Select Books),
Canada (Elizabeth Campbell Books),
Andorra (Llibreria La Puça, La Llibreria).

Orders from bookshops in the UK and elsewhere.

Ebooks
Many of our titles are available also as Ebooks.

www.ingramcontent.com/pod-product-compliance
Lightning Source LLC
Chambersburg PA
CBHW060420090426
42734CB00011B/2381